LOVE

An Essay

By

WILLIAM LYON PHELPS

First published in 1949

British Library Cataloguing-in-Publication Data
A catalogue record for this book is available
from the British Library

CONTENTS

WILLIAM LYON PHELPS

William Lyon Phelps was born on 2nd January 1865, in New Haven, Conneticut, United States.

Phelps earned a B.A. in 1887, writing his thesis on the Idealism of George Berkeley. He then gained an M.A. in 1891 from Yale and his PhD from Harvard in the same year.

During his time a Yale, he offered a course in modern novels which brought the university considerable attention both nationally and internationally. This was quite controversial at the time and Phelps was pressured to give up the course, but eventually, due to popular demand, reinstated it outside the official curriculum.

In 1892, Phelps married Annabel Hubbard, sister of childhood friend Frank Hubbard, and the couple moved to the family estate overlooking Lake Huron. Phelps christened it "The House of the Seven Gables", after the Nathanial Hawthorne story of the same name.

He became a very popular figure at Yale but also as an inspirational orator. He went on lecture tours that drew large audiences, speaking on the virtues of modern literature. He also preached regularly at the Huron City Methodist Episcopal Church and attracted such large crowds that the church was remodelled twice in five years to accommodate them.

Phelps published many essays on modern and European literature, including titles such as *Essays on Modern Novelists* (1910), *Some Makers of American Literature* (1923), and *As I Like it* (1923).

After his retirement from Yale in 1933, after 41 years of service, Phelps continued his public speaking, preaching, and writing a newspaper column. He also sat on book selection committees and acted as a judge for the Pulitzer Prize for literature.

His wife, Annabel, died from a stroke in 1939 and Phelps died four years later, in 1943.

LOVE

NICODEMUS THE Scholar, a man of eminence and authority among the Jews, came to see Jesus by night. Why he chose the night no one knows; perhaps he wished to secure an uninterrupted interview, for during the day the Master was followed by importunate crowds. Possibly he feared some of his acquaintances might see him if he went by day, and he might therefore lose intellectual respect or social prestige. Perhaps he merely wanted a long and revealing talk, believing that the silent hours of the night beget intimacy. Little did the proud Pharisee imagine that when he acted on that impulse and called on the Teacher, he himself would be immortalised; yet such is the fact, for the words spoken on that memorable evening are heard and read today in the farthest corners of the earth.

What Nicodemus himself said is not so often quoted; yet he gave; a description of the Master that has perhaps never been surpassed; a description and a definition on which many Christians with divergent views today might unite. People differ very much as to what place in history should be given to Him, as to whence He came and who He was and as to His credentials.

But Nicodemus said, "We know that thou art a teacher come from God." How did Nicodemus know that? Well, how do we know in talking with a golf professional that he is a Scotsman? How do we know that a man is a Southerner? We know it by his accent, by his manner of speech, sometimes by the expression of his face or the cast of his features. The face and language of Jesus betrayed the country whence He came. The radiance of His countenance, the authoritative and yet tender tones of His voice, showed that the country of His origin was beyond the bounds of earthly geography. He brought into this world a divine atmosphere.

In the first act of the opera Lohengrin, when the solitary and apparently defenceless maiden Elsa is denounced by Telramund, she agrees, somewhat to the general consternation, to submit her cause to the ordeal of trial by combat. The trumpets sound, and there is silence. Who will be her champion? Again the trumpets sound. We hear the thrilling violins, and in the distance we see approaching a knight in silver armour. Elsa calls him the Divine Ambassador, der Gottgesandte; on his face and shining armour is the light that never was on sea or land.

Although Jesus was the ambassador from the kingdom of God to the kingdom of this world, and came to reveal to the children of men His Father's will, He never seemed interested in politics or in forms of government. No political party can claim Him. He was not a Conservative or a Radical, not a Republican or a Democrat or a Socialist. He came not to upset the structure of society, but to appeal to every individual human heart. He turned our sense of values upside down. Every valley shall be exalted, every hill shall be made low; the crooked shall be made straight, and the rough places plain. In this sense He was a revolutionist. He wished to establish a revolution in every individual mind; to change it from cowardice to courage, from slavery to independence, from vulgarity to beauty, from selfishness to unselfishness.

This Teacher who came from God was a specialist; He taught only one subject. The entire course of study contains only three words, but it takes a lifetime to learn it, and only a minority become experts. God is love. As I understand it, this is not intended to be a pretty or sentimental speech. It is not meant to be an optimistic motto, something to hang on the wall of an office, with the hope that it may kindle to renewed activity the flagging spirits of the observer. It is a philosophical principle, a core of thought. The Power whose influence is dimly discerned behind appearances, the Power that holds the stars in their places, the Power that controls the rise and ebb of the tides, the

Power that keeps in accurate running order the mechanism of the universe, that Power is Love.

Hence one who loves God and his fellowmen is in connexion with the motive energy of the universe, with the Supreme Law.

What happens to a person when that idea enters and dominates his mind? Charles Dickens, who understood it better than most novelists, has given us plenty of illustrations, of which we may take one of the most familiar. On the day before Christmas, the financier Scrooge was, even for him, in a particularly unpleasant temper. One is apt to be like that, when one is out of sympathy with the prevailing mood of society. Scrooge in normal weather had the heart of a fish. He was not what we call responsive, demonstrative, expansive. He was acquisitive without being curious; he was not interested in what human beings were actually worth, but only in what they might be worth to him. When he entered a room men felt as one feels on the deck of a ship at night, in the proximity of an iceberg. Every one who met him was chilled and uncomfortable, and his departure brought a sense of relief.

Yet although every one who met him was ill at ease, he was more unhappy than they. They could escape him and his atmosphere; he could not run away from himself. In a dream that night true religion was revealed to him. He was born again. When he opened the window in the morning, the face of the world was changed. He thought it was a marvellous day. He saw a boy crossing the street and he thought him a marvellous boy. What a remarkable, what an unusual boy! His daily life became filled with zest and gusto; everything began to seem exciting, with a tang of adventure. For Scrooge there were no more dull days. Casual strangers on the street saluted him with a smile as of recognition, called forth by his radiant vitality. This is what happens when the love-lesson is learned and put into practice; it should always happen when one really "gets" religion. Scrooge had never imagined there could be such happiness merely in loving. For love is like an efficient furnace that warms every room of a large building.

The scientific evolutionists tell us that it has taken millions and millions of years to change an animal into a man. Love can do that in one second. When that predatory animal, Jean Valjean, stole the candlesticks in the night in the Bishop's House, and was caught next day by the police, they dragged him back to the Bishop's front door, with the evidences of his crime. The Bishop took a look at the wretched creature, and said to the policemen, "Why, I gave him those candlesticks." He lied like a gentleman, like a Christian.

The police are never shocked or puzzled by displays of vice and cruelty; their calloused eyes have looked on human nature at its worst. The only way to shock a policeman is to give him an exhibition of unexpected kindness or generosity. In this instance they were frankly amazed. But the Man of God insisted, and the officers of the law went away shaking their puzzled heads. Then the Bishop put his hand on the dull thief's shoulder and said, "Jean Valjean, my brother! you belong to God now." At that moment divine love entered his heart and changed him from an animal into a man. Love can do this, for it has transforming power. It can change a coward into a hero; it can change a despondent woman into a being full of zest, and it can do it in a moment.

Love is the only genuine test. Two hundred years ago many serious-minded people were agitated by this question-do I or do I not belong to the elect? Am I saved or am I damned? Well, the apostle John has given us in one of his letters a test at once simple and infallible; there can be no possible mistake. We know that we have passed from death unto life because we love the brethren. If we have love in the heart, sincere, unalloyed affection for others, free from hatred or jealousy, without a shade of resentment, then we know we are Christians. It is a searching test.

&nt;   font-family:"Book   Antiqua";mso-fareast-font-family:"MS Mincho"'>A widowed mother was living with her only son; they were the best of comrades, the most intimate of friends. But an adventuress got hold of the young man. She took away his money, his health, his position, his self-respect, and turned him into a vagabond. One day she told him that he must give her a supreme example of his devotion. He must murder his mother and bring to his mistress his mother's bleeding heart. Accordingly the young man went to his mother, killed her, cut the heart from her body, and holding it in his hand, hastened to the evil woman. In his haste he slipped on the pavement and fell headlong. The heart rolled out of his hand. Then the heart spoke and said, "Did you hurt yourself, my dear son?"

If love is the supreme test of Christianity, then it is worse for a church member to show hatred than it is for him to indulge in the grosser vices. If a minister should enter the pulpit quite drunk, it would indeed be scandalous; it would be first-page news. But in reality it would be no worse than for him to show jealousy of other ministers, or to exhibit hatred toward some member of his church. If a deacon should attempt to pass the plate while drunk, it would be an abominable spectacle; but really it ought not to be more shocking than for him not to be "on speaking terms" with another member of the church, or to indulge in slanderous or spiteful or derogatory remarks. Such manifestations of evil are more contrary to the spirit of Christianity than drunkenness, and I have no mind to defend drunkenness.

If two members of the same church are living in hostility, that does not get into the newspapers, because, alas! it is not news. But it is ridiculously inconsistent with their profession. It simply won't do.

The letters of the apostle John show that he was a man of a beautiful and serene temper; but he was called a Son of Thunder. In his first epistle he used two terrible words-liar and murderer. And he was writing to church members.

"If a man say, I love God, and hateth his brother,
he is a liar."

"Whosoever hateth his brother is a murderer."

It is idle to prate about loving God while we have malice in our hearts against our neighbors. It is indeed an absurdity, like a thief praying for success in his undertakings. But how does hatred make one a murderer?

It is really quite simple. Love is a creative force; it sees what is good, brings it out, encourages it, develops it. They say that Love is blind; but it is blind only to defects; it has in reality the sharpest and clearest vision, for it sees beauty where others see only ugliness it sees courage in obscure corners, and ;n commonplace minds it detects and recognizes the seeds of nobility. One cannot become a good critic of music unless one loves music; one will never understand men and women unless one begins by loving them. Perhaps one reason God understands men so perfectly is because He first loves them.

As all this is true of love, so it is true that hatred is desolating, crippling, destructive. Hatred blights everything it touches. It murders the souls of men and women, it destroys their good impulses, their awakening intelligence. If a teacher hates a pupil, he will destroy at birth every impulse to improvement in the pupil's mind, as an icy wind will destroy a tender plant.

In a recent English novel, This Day's Madness, a young girl comes running to her father in a state of excitement; "Oh, father, have you read Matthew Arnold's poem, The Forsaken Merman?" The father was reading the newspaper, and did not wish to be disturbed.

He said impatiently, "Yes, yes," and went on reading. "But, father-" she saw it was no use. That father was a murderer. He blew out the lamp of the girl's mind with the chill wind of indifference. Her soul was just being born, and he trampled on it; because he wanted to read a newspaper. If a little selfish indifference can kill like that, one can easily imagine the destructive power of hatred. We may be murderers.

There is nothing more valuable than the individual human soul. Hatred, resentment, or even indifference, may destroy it. On the other hand, love is not merely a creative force. It is the great preservative. Think of all the women (and men) who are trying vainly to look young; to reduce, to look agile, slender, active, graceful; and the harder they try the more depressing is the result. Yet if they had in their hearts real religion, the principle of love, they would have something eternally fresh. It is the only veritable fountain of youth that so many have sought in vain.

When the good housewives put up fruit in the summer, they do not preserve it with acids. They preserve it with sugar. It takes something sweet to keep things fresh. What is a more unpleasant spectacle than the face of a sour old man or woman, where in addition to the ravages of time, there is the distortion of hate? And what is more beautiful than a face old in years, but alert in intelligence, eager in intellectual curiosity, and shining with benevolence?

> "Nor Spring nor Summer's beauty hath such grace
> As I have seen in one autumnal face."

The apostle John said "No man hath seen God at any time." We come nearest to seeing God when we see love, for where love is, there God is also. There is something inexpressibly sacred in an exhibition of sincere love, as if we were somehow in the presence of God. Two persons who love each other are in a place more holy than the interior of a church.

Tolstoi wrote a short story about a shoemaker, named Martin, who lived and worked in a basement. Out of his narrow window he could see only the boots and shoes of people who passed on the city pavement. Martin grew old. The members of his family were dead, and he was left alone. Like many lonely and forsaken individuals, he turned to the Gospels for relief and balm.

Every night, when the day's work was over, he would light his lamp, and read the words of divine comfort. His heart rose up within him; Jesus and the disciples became his companions. He used to think of the immense happiness of Peter and James and John because they actually saw their Lord day by day. "If

I could only see the Master!" The next morning a poor fellow came into the shop, and it was clear that he was almost perishing with cold and hunger. Martin gave him tea and food and spoke encouraging words. The man went on his way with renewed hope and strength. Later there was the sound of a squabble on the street. Martin went out. A boy had stolen an apple from a poor old applewoman, and there was a fierce exchange of speech. She would have him arrested. Martin made the boy restore the apple, he induced the two antagonists to become friends, and they went away together laughing, the boy carrying the basket. Later he had another opportunity and took it.

That night, in accordance with his custom, Martin lit his lamp, and began to read the Gospels. Soon he was lost in thought. "If I could only see my Master!" Suddenly he felt that he was not alone in the room. He distinctly, heard a voice saying, "Why, Martin, Martin, don't you see Me? I have been with you all the day, long." Then Martin knew that his Saviour had visited him that day, and that he had received Him.

www.ingramcontent.com/pod-product-compliance
Lightning Source LLC
Chambersburg PA
CBHW030106070426
42448CB00037B/1342